NEEDLEPOINT
JOURNAL

Track your projects and record your stitching with this interactive journal

Emma Homent

DAVID & CHARLES
—PUBLISHING—

www.davidandcharles.com

INTRODUCTION

If you're anything like me, you're probably reading this with at least three WIPs on the go; after all, can you really call yourself a stitcher unless you are partway through a whole bunch of creative projects?

We stitchers have a tendency to hoard both canvases and kits. We start a project only to then put it down again as we are seduced by the appeal of another one. And that's totally fine: it's all part of having a creative brain; you have to go where the inspiration takes you. But sometimes this can make it a little tricky to keep track of your stash, or to remember exactly what you did on a finished canvas, and this is where the **Needlepoint Journal** steps in to help.

On each of the design journal pages, you can enter the name of the canvas or kit, who the designer is, when and where you bought it, and even the canvas mesh size. You can record all your hard work and the creative needlepoint choices you made along the way, from the stitches and threads you used, with spaces to catalogue your finishing options and to write notes as you go. This journal will become your perfect stitching companion.

I've even included some of my favourite fancy stitches to give you a little extra inspiration and encouragement to get creative. And there are lots of tips and tricks, fun facts and stitch savvy wisdom too.

And as if that wasn't enough, turning to the back of this journal, you'll find some handy grid pages, together with my advice on how best to approach compensating your stitches. You could even use the grid to invent your own stitches. Oh my word, I would love it if you did!

So dive in and make this journal your own, but most importantly, have fun with it. Needlepoint is an absolute joy of a craft and a brilliant way to escape from the day-to-day grind into a world of endless creativity.

EMMA

WHAT'S THE STITCH?

BYZANTINE STITCH

A dramatic zigzagging stitch that is perfect for covering medium-to-large areas in a hurry. It's quick to work once you have your foundation pattern in place.

+ Working from left to right, bring the needle up at 1 and down through the canvas hole at 2, across two intersections of the canvas. Bring the needle up at 3 and down at 4, and repeat until you have a row of four stitches.

+ Dropping down directly beneath the fourth stitch, work another three diagonal stitches to form a four-stitch column.

+ Then, working from left to right, work another three diagonal stitches to form a four-stitch row.

A lovely zigzag pattern is starting to be formed; continue in this way to fill the desired height.

+ To continue the pattern, work another zigzag alongside your foundation, this time working from right to left over two intersections of the canvas as before.

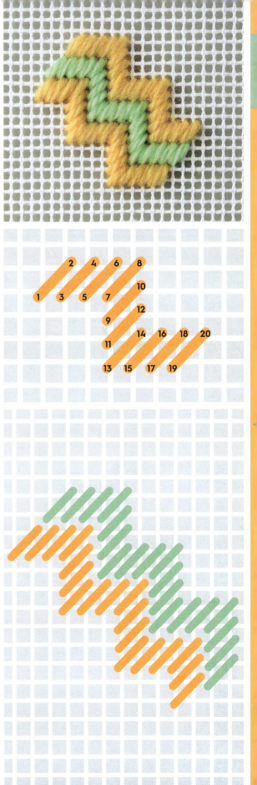

CANVAS/KIT NAME:

Designer:

Purchased from:

Canvas mesh size:

STITCHES:

THREADS:

FINISHING OPTIONS:

NOTES:

FUN FACT: NEEDLEPOINT HAS BEEN A BIG HIT WITH ROYALTY, FROM MARY STUART TO MARIE ANTOINETTE, AND, IN MORE RECENT YEARS, PRINCESS GRACE OF MONACO. SO BASICALLY, YOU'RE A PRINCESS.

CANVAS/KIT NAME:

Designer:

Purchased from:

Canvas mesh size:

STITCHES:

THREADS:

FINISHING OPTIONS:

NOTES:

GET CREATIVE: THERE ARE SO MANY FABULOUS STITCHES TO EXPLORE AND YOU CAN BE THEIR CHAMPION.

CANVAS/KIT NAME:

Designer:

Purchased from:

Canvas mesh size:

STITCHES:

THREADS:

FINISHING OPTIONS:

NOTES:

TIP: DON'T BE TOO WORRIED ABOUT HOW THE BACK OF YOUR NEEDLEPOINT LOOKS, IT'S THE FRONT OF THE PIECE THAT'S IMPORTANT!

CANVAS/KIT NAME:

Designer:

Purchased from:

Canvas mesh size:

STITCHES:

THREADS:

FINISHING OPTIONS:

NOTES:

GET CREATIVE: NEW TO DECORATIVE NEEDLEPOINT STITCHES? PICK A PROJECT WITH EASY-TO-STITCH AREAS, WITH CLEAR GRAPHIC LINES, GEOMETRIC SHAPES AND BIG BLOCKS OF COLOUR.

CANVAS/KIT NAME:

Designer:

Purchased from:

Canvas mesh size:

STITCHES:

THREADS:

FINISHING OPTIONS:

NOTES:

STITCH SAVVY: 12-CT OR 12-HPI CANVAS — WHAT'S THE DIFFERENCE? 'CT' STANDS FOR 'COUNT' AND 'HPI' FOR 'HOLES PER INCH', BUT BOTH MEAN THAT THERE ARE 12 HOLES IN YOUR CANVAS FOR EVERY INCH.

CANVAS/KIT NAME:

Designer:

Purchased from:

Canvas mesh size:

STITCHES:

THREADS:

FINISHING OPTIONS:

NOTES:

TIP: FOR A PERFECT LENGTH OF THREAD TO COMFORTABLY STITCH WITH, HOLD THE END IN YOUR FINGERTIP, STRETCH IT TO THE CROOK OF YOUR ARM, THEN SNIP.

WHAT'S THE STITCH?

HUNGARIAN DIAMOND

A bigger version of Hungarian stitch, this stitch covers much larger areas more quickly.

+ Working from right to left, bring the needle up at 1 and down through the canvas hole at 2, across two bars of canvas.

+ Bring the needle up at 3 and down at 4, across four bars of canvas, then up at 5 and down at 6, across six bars of canvas.

+ Bring the needle up at 7 and down at 8, across four bars of canvas, then up at 9 and down at 10, across two bars of canvas to complete the first Hungarian diamond.

+ Leaving a one canvas hole gap between each set of stitches, continue to stitch Hungarian diamonds until you have a row filling the desired width (11 to 20).

Work each subsequent row in the opposite direction to the one before, evenly fitting the diamonds in between those in the row above (21 to 30).

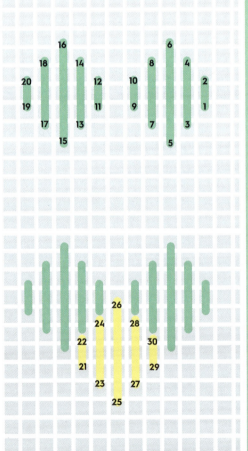

CANVAS/KIT NAME:

Designer: Purchased from:

Canvas mesh size:

STITCHES:

THREADS:

FINISHING OPTIONS:

NOTES:

STITCH SAVVY: STITCHES IN THE HUNGARIAN STITCH FAMILY ARE SOMETIMES CALLED PAVILION STITCHES.

CANVAS/KIT NAME:

Designer:

Purchased from:

Canvas mesh size:

STITCHES:

THREADS:

FINISHING OPTIONS:

NOTES:

WITHOUT YOU, THERE'S JUST CANVAS AND A LOAD OF WOOL. IT DOESN'T EXIST UNTIL YOU STITCH IT. YOUR EFFORT IS AS MUCH A PART OF THE PROCESS AS THE DESIGNER WHO CREATED IT.

CANVAS/KIT NAME:

Designer: Purchased from:

Canvas mesh size:

STITCHES:

THREADS:

FINISHING OPTIONS:

NOTES:

GET CREATIVE: THERE ARE SO MANY USES FOR NEEDLEPOINT EMBROIDERY BEYOND PILLOWS AND PICTURES. NOTEBOOK COVER, WALL HANGING, JEWELLERY— WHAT WILL YOU CHOOSE TO MAKE?

CANVAS/KIT NAME:

Designer:

Purchased from:

Canvas mesh size:

STITCHES:

THREADS:

FINISHING OPTIONS:

NOTES:

TIP: NEEDLE SIZE WILL DEPEND ON THE COUNT OF YOUR CANVAS AND GUIDES ARE READILY AVAILABLE ONLINE, ALTHOUGH YOU MAY CHOOSE TO GO UP OR DOWN A SIZE IF THAT'S MORE COMFORTABLE FOR YOU.

CANVAS/KIT NAME:

Designer:

Purchased from:

Canvas mesh size:

STITCHES:

THREADS:

FINISHING OPTIONS:

NOTES:

FUN FACT: THE FIRST SEWING NEEDLES, USED TENS OF THOUSANDS OF YEARS AGO, WERE MADE FROM BONE AND PLANT THORNS.

CANVAS/KIT NAME:

Designer: Purchased from:

Canvas mesh size:

STITCHES: ## THREADS:

FINISHING OPTIONS: ## NOTES:

TIP: WHEN WORKING MOVEMENT STITCH, CUT THREADS TO DOUBLE YOUR USUAL LENGTH TO SAVE FROM CASTING ON AND OFF TOO OFTEN.

WHAT'S THE STITCH?

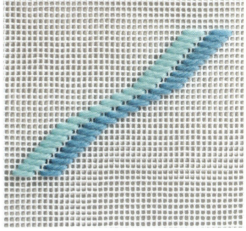

MOVEMENT STITCH

Simple yet effective, the perfectly named movement stitch brings a sense of dynamism to a design, and the more colours you use, the groovier the pattern will be.

+ Working from bottom to top, bring the needle up at 1 and down through the canvas hole at 2, going across four bars of canvas. Bring the needle up at 3 and down at 4, again across four bars of canvas, this time stepping one hole to the right. Repeat to stitch a total of nine stitches.

+ Now taking a two hole step to the right, bring the needle up at 5 and down at 6, across four bars of canvas. Repeat to stitch a total of seven stitches like this. Continue in this way until you have a column filling the desired height.

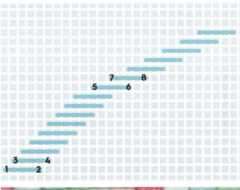

CANVAS/KIT NAME:

Designer:

Purchased from:

Canvas mesh size:

STITCHES:

THREADS:

FINISHING OPTIONS:

NOTES:

STITCH SAVVY: THE USE OF A FRAME GIVES THE CANVAS AN EVEN TENSION, MAKING IT EASIER TO STITCH; A TAUT CANVAS ALLOWS YOUR NEEDLE TO SLIP THROUGH THE CANVAS HOLES REALLY SMOOTHLY.

CANVAS/KIT NAME:

Designer:

Purchased from:

Canvas mesh size:

STITCHES:

THREADS:

FINISHING OPTIONS:

NOTES:

GET CREATIVE: USE THE CANVAS EDGE TO SWATCH-TEST YOUR STITCHES, TO SEE HOW DIFFERENT STITCHES WILL LOOK ALONGSIDE EACH OTHER BEFORE YOU COMMIT THEM TO THE DESIGN.

CANVAS/KIT NAME:

Designer:

Purchased from:

Canvas mesh size:

STITCHES:

THREADS:

FINISHING OPTIONS:

NOTES:

STITCH SAVVY: THERE ARE DIFFERENT TYPES OF FRAME TO CHOOSE FROM, INCLUDING SCROLL FRAMES, BAR FRAMES AND CLIP FRAMES.

CANVAS/KIT NAME:

Designer:

Purchased from:

Canvas mesh size:

STITCHES:

THREADS:

FINISHING OPTIONS:

NOTES:

TIP: YOUR CHOICE OF FRAME WILL DEPEND ON WHAT FEELS RIGHT WITH HOW YOU STITCH, SO BORROW A FRIEND'S AND TRY BEFORE YOU BUY.

CANVAS/KIT NAME:

Designer:

Purchased from:

Canvas mesh size:

STITCHES:

THREADS:

FINISHING OPTIONS:

NOTES:

DID YOU ENJOY THIS DESIGN? ARE YOU PROUD OF YOURSELF? WHAT WOULD YOU CHANGE NEXT TIME?

CANVAS/KIT NAME:

Designer:

Purchased from:

Canvas mesh size:

STITCHES:

THREADS:

FINISHING OPTIONS:

NOTES:

TIP: A BIG CANVAS CAN BE A LITTLE OVERWHELMING SOMETIMES. TAKE TIME OUT BETWEEN BIGGER PROJECTS WITH A QUICK-TO-STITCH MINI, SUCH AS A LITTLE HANGING ORNAMENT PERHAPS?

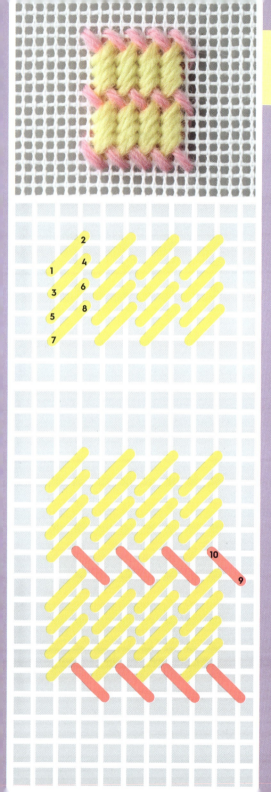

WHAT'S THE STITCH?

CONNECTED CASHMERE STITCH

A lesser known member of the cashmere stitch family, this beautiful stitch looks especially effective when worked in two colours.

+ Working from top to bottom, bring the needle up at 1 and down through the canvas hole at 2, across two canvas intersections.

+ Bring the needle up at 3 and down at 4, up at 5 and down at 6, up at 7 and down at 8 to complete one block made with four parallel diagonal stitches.

+ Continue to work these blocks across the row to fill the width of your canvas.

+ To work the row that will 'connect' the rows of cashmere stitch blocks, you will be working from right to left. Bring the needle up at 9 and down through the canvas hole at 10, across two intersections of the canvas.

Continue along the row to add a little 'tail' to each of the cashmere stitch blocks, as shown on the diagram.

+ Continue to work these two rows down the canvas until you have filled the desired height.

CANVAS/KIT NAME:

Designer:

Purchased from:

Canvas mesh size:

STITCHES:

THREADS:

FINISHING OPTIONS:

NOTES:

STITCH SAVVY: THERE ARE MANY VARIATION STITCHES TO EXPLORE IN THE CASHMERE STITCH FAMILY, ALL FEATURING AND EXPERIMENTING WITH A RECTANGULAR BLOCK SHAPE.

CANVAS/KIT NAME:

Designer:

Purchased from:

Canvas mesh size:

STITCHES:

THREADS:

FINISHING OPTIONS:

NOTES:

TIP: WHEN MAKING YOUR STITCHES, YOU DON'T NEED TO PULL YOUR TAPESTRY WOOL TIGHTLY, BUT JUST ENOUGH TO MAKE SURE THE STITCH ISN'T BAGGY.

CANVAS/KIT NAME:

Designer: Purchased from:

Canvas mesh size:

STITCHES: ## THREADS:

FINISHING OPTIONS: ## NOTES:

STITCH SAVVY: EACH STITCH SHOULD FIT SNUGGLY AGAINST THE CANVAS. YOU'LL SOON GET INTO A RHYTHM WITH IT AND IT WILL BECOME VERY RELAXING.

CANVAS/KIT NAME:

Designer:

Purchased from:

Canvas mesh size:

STITCHES:

THREADS:

FINISHING OPTIONS:

NOTES:

TIP: IF A PROJECT REQUIRES MORE THAN ONE SKEIN OF THE SAME COLOUR, BE SURE TO USE THE SAME DYE LOT NUMBER, OTHERWISE YOU'LL SPOT THE DIFFERENCE WHEN YOU START STITCHING!

CANVAS/KIT NAME:

Designer: Purchased from:

Canvas mesh size:

STITCHES: ## THREADS:

FINISHING OPTIONS: ## NOTES:

DON'T BE AFRAID TO EXPERIMENT WITH STITCHES.
SURE, YOU'LL MAKE THE ODD MISTAKE, BUT IT'S ALL
PART OF THE FUN. SO BE BOLD, AND BE BRAVE!

CANVAS/KIT NAME:

Designer:

Purchased from:

Canvas mesh size:

STITCHES:

THREADS:

FINISHING OPTIONS:

NOTES:

GET CREATIVE: PINWHEEL STITCH, SHELL STITCH, SCALLOP STITCH AND DRAGONFLY STITCH ARE JUST A FEW OF THE MANY 'SHAPED' STITCHES TO BE DISCOVERED.

WHAT'S THE STITCH?

PINWHEEL STITCH

Pinwheel stitch only really works in medium-to-large areas, but a single pinwheel is an eye-catching feature wherever it's placed.

Working each quarter of the pinwheel in turn, start with the bottom right-hand section first, then move in a clockwise direction.

- Bring the needle up at 1 and down through the canvas hole at 2, across seven bars of canvas, up at 3 and down at 4, across five bars of canvas, up at 5 and down at 6 across three bars of canvas, up at 7 and down at 8, across one bar of canvas.

- Now working a triangle shape in a different direction over the top of your stitches, bring the needle up at 9 and down at 2, up at 10 and down at 11, up at 12 and down at 13, up at 14 and down at 15.

- To start the next quarter of the pinwheel, bring the needle up through the canvas hole at 16 ready to bring it back down at 2, across seven bars of canvas.

- Work the remaining quarters in the same way, using 2 as your centre point as you move around clockwise.

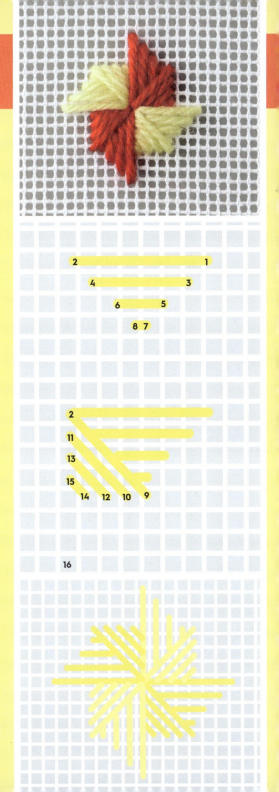

CANVAS/KIT NAME:

Designer:

Purchased from:

Canvas mesh size:

STITCHES:

THREADS:

FINISHING OPTIONS:

NOTES:

GET CREATIVE: YOU CAN TAKE ANY DESIGN AND PUT YOUR OWN CREATIVE SPIN ON IT BY CHOOSING THE STITCHES THAT EXCITE YOU.

CANVAS/KIT NAME:

Designer:

Purchased from:

Canvas mesh size:

STITCHES:

THREADS:

FINISHING OPTIONS:

NOTES:

STITCH SAVVY: DON'T USE AN EMBROIDERY HOOP FOR NEEDLEPOINT! IT WILL BUCKLE YOUR CANVAS WITHOUT PROVIDING THE EVEN TENSION YOU REQUIRE.

CANVAS/KIT NAME:

Designer:

Purchased from:

Canvas mesh size:

STITCHES:

THREADS:

FINISHING OPTIONS:

NOTES:

STITCH SAVVY: TENT STITCH, CONTINENTAL STITCH AND BASKETWEAVE STITCH MAY ALL LOOK THE SAME FROM THE TOP BUT THEY WORK THEIR WAY IN AND OUT OF THE CANVAS IN SLIGHTLY DIFFERENT WAYS.

CANVAS/KIT NAME:

Designer:

Purchased from:

Canvas mesh size:

STITCHES:

THREADS:

FINISHING OPTIONS:

NOTES:

GET CREATIVE: WHY NOT ADD A DIFFERENT STITCH TO YOUR REPERTOIRE EACH WEEK? CHECK OUT #STITCHMONDAYS ON INSTAGRAM FOR A WEEKLY SHOWCASE OF NEEDLEPOINT STITCHES.

CANVAS/KIT NAME:

Designer:

Purchased from:

Canvas mesh size:

STITCHES:

THREADS:

FINISHING OPTIONS:

NOTES:

STITCH SAVVY: IT'S IMPORTANT TO FIND A COMPATIBLE FIT BETWEEN THE THREAD YOU CHOOSE TO STITCH WITH AND THE CANVAS COUNT YOU'RE STITCHING ONTO.

CANVAS/KIT NAME:

Designer:

Purchased from:

Canvas mesh size:

STITCHES:

THREADS:

FINISHING OPTIONS:

NOTES:

TIP: IF SUBSTITUTING ONE THREAD BRAND FOR ANOTHER, DO CHECK LENGTH AS THIS MAY NOT BE THE SAME, AND YOU DON'T WANT TO RUN OUT OF THREAD WITH JUST A SMALL SECTION LEFT TO STITCH!

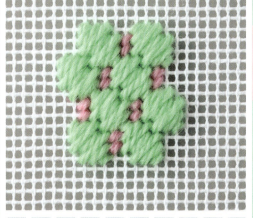

WHAT'S THE STITCH?

SOUFFLE STITCH

This diagonally worked stitch ripples across the canvas, making it perfect for stitching sections of sea or sky.

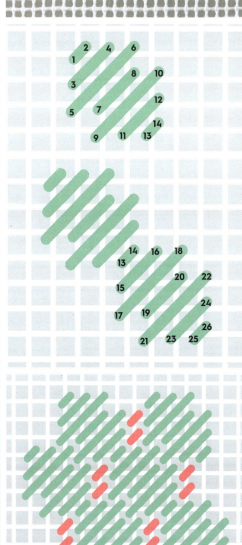

+ Working from top to bottom, bring the needle up at 1 and down at 2, across one intersection of canvas, up at 3 and down at 4, across two intersections of canvas, up at 5 and down at 6, across three intersections of canvas, up at 7 and down at 8, across two intersections of canvas, up at 9 and down at 10, across three intersections of canvas, up at 11 and down at 12, across two intersections of canvas, and up at 13 and down at 14, across one intersection of canvas.

+ Continue in this way until you have a diagonal row of stitches filling the desired height.

Note that the stitch marked 13 to 14 becomes the first stitch for the next run of souffle stitch.

+ Work all the rows of souffle stitch first to fill the desired width.

Note how the souffle stitch rows slot in well next to each other but how a little gap is left for the tent stitch flourishes (pink here) to be added at the end.

+ Finally, fill the gaps in between the souffle stitch rows with tent stitch.

CANVAS/KIT NAME:

Designer:

Purchased from:

Canvas mesh size:

STITCHES:

THREADS:

FINISHING OPTIONS:

NOTES:

FUN FACT: TENT STITCH IS PROBABLY THE FIRST NEEDLEPOINT STITCH YOU LEARNT, BUT DID YOU KNOW THAT THE ANCIENT EGYPTIANS USED THESE SIMPLE, SMALL DIAGONAL STITCHES TO SEW UP THEIR TENTS?

CANVAS/KIT NAME:

Designer:

Purchased from:

Canvas mesh size:

STITCHES:

THREADS:

FINISHING OPTIONS:

NOTES:

FUN FACT: THE NEEDLEPOINT SAMPLER BECAME POPULAR IN THE 18TH CENTURY AS A WAY TO SHOW OFF DIFFERENT STITCH TECHNIQUES IN A SINGLE PIECE OF WORK.

CANVAS/KIT NAME:

Designer: Purchased from:

Canvas mesh size:

STITCHES:

THREADS:

FINISHING OPTIONS:

NOTES:

GET CREATIVE: TAKE A PIECE OF BLANK CANVAS AND MARK OUT SOME SQUARES TO FILL WITH DECORATIVE STITCHES. IT'S A GREAT WAY TO DISCOVER YOUR PERSONAL FAVOURITES.

CANVAS/KIT NAME:

Designer:

Purchased from:

Canvas mesh size:

STITCHES:

THREADS:

FINISHING OPTIONS:

NOTES:

TIP: WORKING ON A LARGE PROJECT? CUT ALL YOUR THREAD LENGTHS IN ONE GO, AND KEEP THEM ON A THREAD ORGANIZER OR ON LARGE BOBBINS UNTIL YOU NEED THEM.

CANVAS/KIT NAME:

Designer: Purchased from:

Canvas mesh size:

STITCHES: ## THREADS:

FINISHING OPTIONS: ## NOTES:

YOUR STITCHING REFLECTS HOW YOU ARE FEELING IN THE MOMENT, SO CELEBRATE THE IMPERFECTIONS.

CANVAS/KIT NAME:

Designer:

Purchased from:

Canvas mesh size:

STITCHES:

THREADS:

FINISHING OPTIONS:

NOTES:

IS THERE AN OPPORTUNITY TO INCORPORATE NEW NEEDLEPOINT STITCHES INTO THIS DESIGN?

CANVAS/KIT NAME:

Designer: Purchased from:

Canvas mesh size:

STITCHES: ## THREADS:

FINISHING OPTIONS: ## NOTES:

GET CREATIVE: HAVE FUN FINDING JUST THE RIGHT STITCH FOR THE TEXTURES OF EVERYDAY THINGS, FROM THE READY-TO-BE DIPPED YOLK OF A FRIED EGG, TO THE PUFFINESS OF A CLOUD.

CANVAS/KIT NAME:

Designer:

Purchased from:

Canvas mesh size:

STITCHES:

THREADS:

FINISHING OPTIONS:

NOTES:

FUN FACT: SOMETIMES A PROJECT NEEDS A BIT OF IMPACT AND STRUCTURED MOVEMENT. THERE ARE LOTS OF STEPPING STITCHES TO EXPLORE, BUT JACQUARD STITCH IS ONE OF MY FAVOURITES.

WHAT'S THE STITCH?

JACQUARD STITCH

If you're looking for a stepped stitch with a bit more impact, look no further!

+ Working from bottom to top, bring the needle up at 1 and down through the canvas hole at 2, going across one intersection of canvas. Then up at 3 and down at 4, again across one intersection. Repeat until you have nine small diagonal stitches worked one directly above the other, then work four stitches in a horizontal row to the left, up at 5 and down at 6, up at 7 and down at 8, up at 9 and down at 10, up at 11 and down at 12.

+ Continue in this way until you've filled the height of your canvas area.

Now to work a band of wider diagonal stitches. This has most impact when worked in a second colour.

+ Working from bottom to top, bring the needle up at 13 and down through the canvas hole at 14, across three intersections of canvas, up at 15 and down at 16, and continue to stitch a long diagonal stitch alongside each of the small stitches.

Repeat to stitch narrow and wide columns of diagonal stitches to continue the pattern across the canvas.

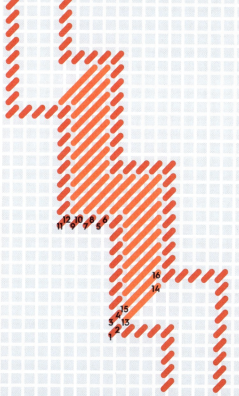

CANVAS/KIT NAME:

Designer: Purchased from:

Canvas mesh size:

STITCHES: THREADS:

FINISHING OPTIONS: NOTES:

STITCH SAVVY: FILLING STITCHES ARE THE STITCHES YOU CHOOSE TO FILL A SPECIFICALLY SHAPED AREA OF YOUR NEEDLEPOINT DESIGN.

CANVAS/KIT NAME:

Designer:

Purchased from:

Canvas mesh size:

STITCHES:

THREADS:

FINISHING OPTIONS:

NOTES:

GET CREATIVE: LOOKING FOR STITCHES TO REPLICATE FEATHERS ON A DESIGN FEATURING BIRDS? CHECK OUT STAGGERED HALF DIAMOND RAY STITCH, DAMASK STITCH, OR THE APTLY NAMED WING STITCH.

CANVAS/KIT NAME:

Designer:

Purchased from:

Canvas mesh size:

STITCHES:

THREADS:

FINISHING OPTIONS:

NOTES:

TIP: NEVER USE A MIX OF THREAD BRANDS FOR THE SAME COLOURED AREA OF A DESIGN: EACH HAS A DIFFERENT DYEING PROFILE AND WHEN PLACED ALONGSIDE EACH OTHER, YOU'LL SEE SUBTLETIES IN TONE.

CANVAS/KIT NAME:

Designer:

Purchased from:

Canvas mesh size:

STITCHES:

THREADS:

FINISHING OPTIONS:

NOTES:

GET CREATIVE: WHEN CHOOSING STITCHES FOR YOUR BACKGROUND, DON'T LET THEM PULL THE FOCUS FROM YOUR MAIN DESIGN AREA.

CANVAS/KIT NAME:

Designer:

Purchased from:

Canvas mesh size:

STITCHES:

THREADS:

FINISHING OPTIONS:

NOTES:

STITCH SAVVY: FULL COVERAGE, WHERE STITCHES COMPLETELY COVER THE CANVAS, IS THE KIT NORM, BUT IF YOU USE DECORATIVE STITCHES WITH INTERMITTENT COVERAGE YOU CAN PLAY WITH TEXTURE.

CANVAS/KIT NAME:

Designer: Purchased from:

Canvas mesh size:

STITCHES: ## THREADS:

FINISHING OPTIONS: ## NOTES:

GET CREATIVE: EXPLORE THE WORLD OF METALLIC THREADS TO ADD A BIT OF GLITZ AND LIGHT-CATCHING SPARKLE TO YOUR PROJECTS.

WHAT'S THE STITCH?

BARGELLO CREST

You'll need a large area of canvas to show this off properly. This can look complicated to do, but like all things stitch, just establish a starting line and the rest falls into place.

- Working from left to right, bring the needle up at 1 and down through the canvas hole at 2, across three intersections of canvas. Stepping up one canvas hole each time, bring the needle up at 3 and down at 4, repeating eight times to make a total of nine stitches ending with the stitch marked 5 to 6.

- Then bring the needle up at 7 and down at 8, alongside the stitch marked 5 to 6, and make another three parallel diagonal stitches, as shown in the diagram.

- Now stepping down one canvas hole, make two parallel diagonal stitches, 9 and 10 and 11 and 12. Repeat to make two more identical pairs of stitches.

- Stepping down one canvas hole, bring the needle up at 13 and down at 14, and up at 15 and down at 16 to complete the Bargello crest.

- Stitch 15 to 16 becomes stitch 1 to 2 of the next Bargello crest in the row as you continue to repeat this pattern across the row.

Note that all the stitches are worked across three intersections of the canvas.

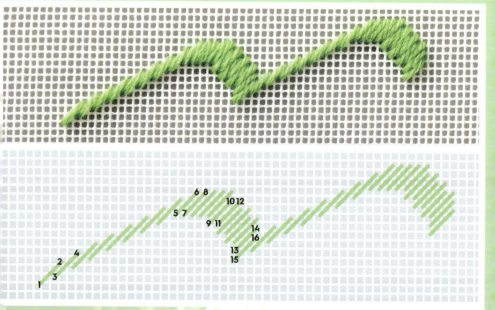

CANVAS/KIT NAME:

Designer: Purchased from:

Canvas mesh size:

STITCHES: ## THREADS:

FINISHING OPTIONS: ## NOTES:

FUN FACT: BARGELLO IS A SUB-GROUP OF NEEDLEPOINT STITCHES THAT DATE BACK TO THE 17TH CENTURY. THEY WERE NAMED AFTER THE PALACE IN FLORENCE IN WHICH THEY WERE FOUND ADORNING CHAIRS.

CANVAS/KIT NAME:

Designer:

Purchased from:

Canvas mesh size:

STITCHES:

THREADS:

FINISHING OPTIONS:

NOTES:

SHARE YOUR STITCHING IDEAS WITH STITCHING FRIENDS IN PERSON AND ONLINE, AND SUPPORT EACH OTHER. ENJOY CRAFTING TOGETHER.

CANVAS/KIT NAME:

Designer:

Purchased from:

Canvas mesh size:

STITCHES:

THREADS:

FINISHING OPTIONS:

NOTES:

TIP: A PAIR OF 'SNIPS', WHICH LOOK LIKE MINI SHEEP SHEARS, ARE AN INCREASINGLY POPULAR ALTERNATIVE TO EMBROIDERY SCISSORS.

CANVAS/KIT NAME:

Designer:

Purchased from:

Canvas mesh size:

STITCHES:

THREADS:

FINISHING OPTIONS:

NOTES:

FUN FACT: WHY IS REMOVING AN AREA OF INCORRECT STITCHING WITH A SEAM UNPICKER CALLED 'FROGGING'? BECAUSE YOU 'RIP IT, RIP IT'!

CANVAS/KIT NAME:

Designer:

Purchased from:

Canvas mesh size:

STITCHES:

THREADS:

FINISHING OPTIONS:

NOTES:

TIP: IF YOUR THREAD COMES IN SKEINS OR HANKS, TAKE OFF THE PAPER BAND FIRST BEFORE PULLING THE END, OTHERWISE YOU'LL GET CAUGHT UP IN A BIG TANGLY MESS!

CANVAS/KIT NAME:

Designer:

Purchased from:

Canvas mesh size:

STITCHES:

THREADS:

FINISHING OPTIONS:

NOTES:

GET CREATIVE: TO ADD A STEM TO LEAF STITCH, BRING THE NEEDLE UP THROUGH THE HOLE AT THE BOTTOM CENTRE OF THE LEAF SHAPE, THEN DOWN AGAIN AT THE BASE OF THE STITCH THAT SITS AT THE TOP.

WHAT'S THE STITCH?

LEAF STITCH

Leaf stitch is perfect for medium-to-large areas and works well as a background stitch.

- Starting at the left-hand side of the area to be stitched, bring the needle up at 1 and down through the canvas hole at 2, across four intersections of canvas but stepping to the left across three bars only, then bring the needle up at 3 and down at 4, up at 5 and down at 6.

- The next two stitches are also worked across four intersections of canvas but with a steeper slant: bring the needle up at 7 and down at 8, stepping to the left across two bars, and up at 9 and down at 10, stepping to the left across one bar. The top stitch is worked vertically across three bars of canvas, bringing the needle up at 11 and down at 12.

- Working down the other side, mirror the stitches to complete the leaf.

- To continue the row, line up the other leaves in your row so they all sit at the same height as the first leaf stitch.

- For the next row, fit the leaf stitches in between those on the row above.

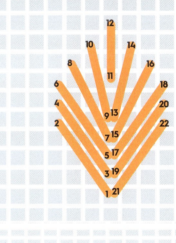

CANVAS/KIT NAME:

Designer:

Purchased from:

Canvas mesh size:

STITCHES:

THREADS:

FINISHING OPTIONS:

NOTES:

STITCH SAVVY: 'TRAVELLING A THREAD' IS TAKING IT ACROSS THE BACK OF YOUR WORK TO A NEW STARTING POSITION, BUT DON'T BE TEMPTED TO TRAVEL IT TOO FAR OR ACROSS UNSTITCHED CANVAS.

CANVAS/KIT NAME:

Designer: Purchased from:

Canvas mesh size:

STITCHES: ## THREADS:

FINISHING OPTIONS: ## NOTES:

GET CREATIVE: WHILE MOST KITS STILL COME PACKAGED WITH WOOL, THESE DAYS ANY FIBRE CAN FIND ITS PLACE ON A NEEDLEPOINT CANVAS — EVEN RIBBON!

CANVAS/KIT NAME:

Designer:

Purchased from:

Canvas mesh size:

STITCHES:

THREADS:

FINISHING OPTIONS:

NOTES:

TIP: PLASTIC CANVAS IS A POURED AND STAMPED PIECE OF SOFT, FLEXIBLE PLASTIC THAT HOLDS ITS SHAPE PERFECTLY, MAKING IT A GREAT CHOICE FOR THOSE JUST STARTING TO LEARN NEEDLEPOINT.

CANVAS/KIT NAME:

Designer:

Purchased from:

Canvas mesh size:

STITCHES:

THREADS:

FINISHING OPTIONS:

NOTES:

STITCH SAVVY: CROSS STITCH MAY BE THE BEST-KNOWN STITCH, YET THERE ARE MORE FAMILY MEMBERS TO EXPLORE, SUCH AS UPRIGHT CROSS STITCH, DOUBLE CROSS STITCH AND OBLONG CROSS STITCH.

CANVAS/KIT NAME:

Designer:

Purchased from:

Canvas mesh size:

STITCHES:

THREADS:

FINISHING OPTIONS:

NOTES:

STITCH SAVVY: TAPESTRY WOOL IS SPUN WITH A PARTICULARLY DENSE TWIST, WHICH MAKES IT A LOT LESS STRETCHY THAN KNITTING YARN.

CANVAS/KIT NAME:

Designer:

Purchased from:

Canvas mesh size:

STITCHES:

THREADS:

FINISHING OPTIONS:

NOTES:

FUN FACT: NEEDLEPOINT, ALONG WITH OTHER HANDS-ON CRAFTS, HAS BEEN PROVEN TO BE A MOOD BOOSTER! WHAT BETTER REASON COULD THERE BE TO PICK UP YOUR NEEDLE?

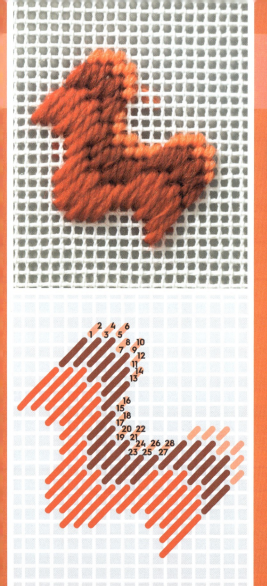

WHAT'S THE STITCH?

BARGELLO WAVE STITCH

At first glance this stitch can look a bit tricky, but as it's worked on perfect diagonals it's actually incredibly easy. Once you have your first row of stitches, you'll be flying through it.

+ The first row is worked in tent stitch and establishes the flow of the pattern. Working from top to bottom, bring the needle up at 1 and down through the canvas hole at 2, across one intersection of canvas. Create two more parallel stitches, 3 to 4, 5 to 6. Then step down a canvas hole to work 7 to 8, and 9 to 10. Step down a canvas hole for 11 to 12, and step down again for 13 to 14.

+ Now, bring the needle up at 15 and down at 16, and continue to follow the stitching path as shown on the diagram. You are basically working the first run of stitches (1 to 14) to reverse the shape, finishing by bringing the needle up at 27 and down at 28. Notice that there is a one bar gap in between the top (curve) and the bottom (dip) line of stitches. Continue to alternate these curve and dip sections of tent stitch until you have reached the desired height and width of your canvas.

+ For the second row, line up your stitches with your first row of stitches, working across two intersections of canvas. For the third row, line up your stitches with your second row of stitches, this time working across three intersections of canvas. Continue across your canvas repeating these three rows.

If you're in the mood to experiment, try varying the order of the row. It can look impressive worked 1- 2 - 3 - 2 - 1, for example.

CANVAS/KIT NAME:

Designer:

Purchased from:

Canvas mesh size:

STITCHES:

THREADS:

FINISHING OPTIONS:

NOTES:

STITCH SAVVY: TRADITIONALLY WORKED ONLY WITH UPRIGHT LONG STITCHES, TODAY'S BARGELLO DESIGNERS NOW WORK THEIR STITCHES IN MULTIPLE DIRECTIONS ACROSS THE CANVAS!

CANVAS/KIT NAME:

Designer:

Purchased from:

Canvas mesh size:

STITCHES:

THREADS:

FINISHING OPTIONS:

NOTES:

STITCH SAVVY: 'PARKING THREAD' IS TAKING YOUR THREAD TO THE FRONT OF YOUR STITCHING AND LEAVING IT IN PLACE, OUT OF THE WAY, READY TO BE PICKED UP AGAIN WHEN IT IS NEEDED.

CANVAS/KIT NAME:

Designer:

Purchased from:

Canvas mesh size:

STITCHES:

THREADS:

FINISHING OPTIONS:

NOTES:

GET CREATIVE: EXPERIMENT WITH DIFFERENT STITCHES TO CREATE DIFFERENT TEXTURES. SWAP THEM OUT FOR THOSE IN THE KITS YOU BUY OR THE PROJECTS YOU MAKE.

CANVAS/KIT NAME:

Designer:

Purchased from:

Canvas mesh size:

STITCHES:

THREADS:

FINISHING OPTIONS:

NOTES:

FUN FACT: MONTHLY IN-PERSON OR ZOOM-BASED STITCH CLUBS ARE A BRILLIANT WAY TO MEET UP WITH LIKE-MINDED PEOPLE TO SHOW OFF YOUR WIPS.

CANVAS/KIT NAME:

Designer: Purchased from:

Canvas mesh size:

STITCHES: THREADS:

FINISHING OPTIONS: NOTES:

GET CREATIVE: PLOT YOUR WAY AROUND YOUR CANVAS, CHECKING AREAS THAT OVERLAP TO MAKE SURE YOU DON'T UNINTENTIONALLY ADD TOO MUCH CONTRAST WHEN INTRODUCING NEW STITCHES.

CANVAS/KIT NAME:

Designer: Purchased from:

Canvas mesh size:

STITCHES: **THREADS:**

FINISHING OPTIONS: **NOTES:**

GET CREATIVE: DAVID STITCH IS GREAT FOR FILLING LARGE AREAS OF CANVAS, ALTHOUGH THERE ARE PLENTY OF OTHER STITCHES YOU CAN CHOOSE TOO, INCLUDING WOVEN RIBBONS AND VEE STITCH.

WHAT'S THE STITCH?

DAVID STITCH

If you are looking for a statement stitch that can cover a large area quickly, then David stitch might just be what you have been searching for.

+ Bring the needle up at 1 and down through the canvas hole at 2, across eight intersections of canvas, up at 3 and down at 4, up at 5 and down at 6, to form the first half of the stitch.

+ Bring the needle up through the canvas hole at 7 and follow the order of the stitches to work a mirror image of the first half of the stitch.

+ Continue to work David stitches, fitting them together as shown on the diagram.

+ The gap at the centre of the David stitch pattern can be neatly filled with an upright cross stitch.

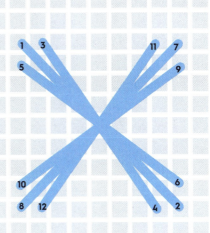

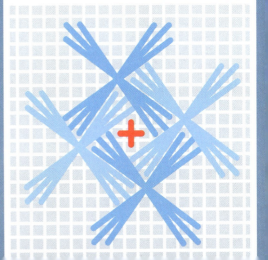

CANVAS/KIT NAME:

Designer:

Purchased from:

Canvas mesh size:

STITCHES:

THREADS:

FINISHING OPTIONS:

NOTES:

STITCH SAVVY: 'COMPENSATING' STITCHES MAY BE NECESSARY TO NEATLY FINISH RIGHT UP TO THE EDGE OF A SHAPED SECTION AND IT INVOLVES ADAPTING THE WORKING OF THE STITCH TO DO JUST THAT.

CANVAS/KIT NAME:

Designer:

Purchased from:

Canvas mesh size:

STITCHES:

THREADS:

FINISHING OPTIONS:

NOTES:

TIP: WHEN CASTING OFF, RUN THE THREAD THROUGH THE BACKS OF STITCHES OF THE SAME COLOUR WHEREVER POSSIBLE, IN ORDER TO PREVENT SHOW-THROUGH ON THE FRONT OF THE PIECE.

CANVAS/KIT NAME:

Designer:

Purchased from:

Canvas mesh size:

STITCHES:

THREADS:

FINISHING OPTIONS:

NOTES:

STITCH SAVVY: WHEN COMPENSATING STITCHES, TENT STITCH IS LIKELY TO BECOME YOUR BEST FRIEND!

CANVAS/KIT NAME:

Designer: Purchased from:

Canvas mesh size:

STITCHES:

THREADS:

FINISHING OPTIONS:

NOTES:

TIP: OPEN WEAVE CANVAS CAN FEEL STIFF IN YOUR HAND, BUT DON'T WORRY — IT WILL BECOME SOFTER AS YOU WORK.

CANVAS/KIT NAME:

Designer:

Purchased from:

Canvas mesh size:

STITCHES:

THREADS:

FINISHING OPTIONS:

NOTES:

FUN FACT: IF YOU CAN FIND ANYTHING WITH AN EVEN SET OF HOLES ACROSS IT, YOU'LL FIND A CRAFTER PREPARED TO STITCH IT. CHAIN-LINK FENCES MAKE FOR EXCELLENT STITCH INSTALLATIONS!

CANVAS/KIT NAME:

Designer:

Purchased from:

Canvas mesh size:

STITCHES:

THREADS:

FINISHING OPTIONS:

NOTES:

GET CREATIVE: VARIEGATED THREADS ARE DYED IN VARYING COLOURS OR IN TONAL SHADES OF ONE COLOUR. STITCHING WITH THEM IS A BIT LIKE PAINTING AND, BOY, DO THEY WORK WELL FOR SKIES!

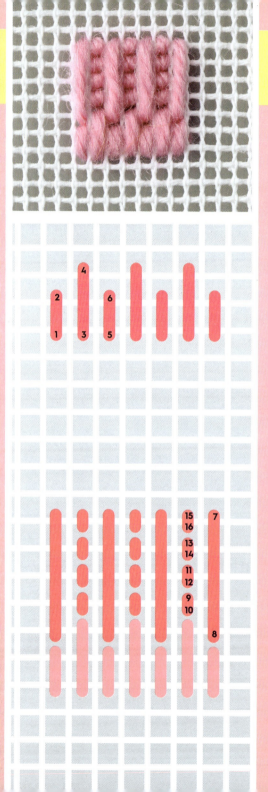

WHAT'S THE STITCH?

ART DECO STITCH

The graphic shape of this recently invented stitch is reminiscent of Art Deco buildings. It is brilliant for medium-to-large areas and for narrow vertical strips.

+ Working from left to right, bring the needle up at 1 and down through the canvas hole at 2, across two bars of canvas.

+ Bring the needle back up at 3 and down at 4, across three bars of canvas. Continue in this way until you have a row filling the desired width.

The bottom half of the pattern is now complete; your stitches align at the base line but alternate in length at the top line.

+ Working in the opposite direction to start the top half of the pattern, bring the needle up at 7 and down at 8, across five bars of canvas. In the next column, work four vertical backstitches: up at 9 and down at 10, up at 11 and down at 12, up at 13 and down at 14, up at 15 and down at 16.

+ Continue alternating these two stitch columns to fill the desired width.

CANVAS/KIT NAME:

Designer:

Purchased from:

Canvas mesh size:

STITCHES:

THREADS:

FINISHING OPTIONS:

NOTES:

GET CREATIVE: NEW STITCHES ARE BEING DEVISED ALL THE TIME. TAKE AS AN EXAMPLE THE ART DECO STITCH, INVENTED IN 2021 BY SHARON GORDON MENSING.

CANVAS/KIT NAME:

Designer:

Purchased from:

Canvas mesh size:

STITCHES:

THREADS:

FINISHING OPTIONS:

NOTES:

TIP: LOOKING FOR A SHARED STITCHING EXPERIENCE? THEN SALS, SHORT FOR 'STITCH-ALONGS', WHERE STITCHERS GET THE SAME DESIGN AND WORK ON IT SIMULTANEOUSLY, COULD BE JUST THE THING FOR YOU.

CANVAS/KIT NAME:

Designer:

Purchased from:

Canvas mesh size:

STITCHES:

THREADS:

FINISHING OPTIONS:

NOTES:

GET CREATIVE: ADD DETAIL TO A STITCHED SKY BACKGROUND WITH A RANGE OF STAR-EFFECT STITCHES, INCLUDING STAR STITCH (AKA ALGERIAN EYE STITCH), DUTCH STITCH AND EYELET STARS.

CANVAS/KIT NAME:

Designer:

Purchased from:

Canvas mesh size:

STITCHES:

THREADS:

FINISHING OPTIONS:

NOTES:

TIP: INVEST IN A PROJECT BAG TO KEEP YOUR CANVAS AND THREADS NEAT AND FLUFF-FREE BETWEEN STITCH SESSIONS. SCOOP UP ALL YOUR NOTIONS INTO IT, TOO, SO THAT YOU HAVE EVERYTHING TO HAND.

CANVAS/KIT NAME:

Designer:

Purchased from:

Canvas mesh size:

STITCHES:

THREADS:

FINISHING OPTIONS:

NOTES:

STITCH SAVVY: IF YOU HAVEN'T USED A FRAME, IT'S PERFECTLY NORMAL TO FIND THAT YOUR STITCHED CANVAS IS A LITTLE DISTORTED. THIS IS EASILY FIXED BY A PROCESS KNOWN AS 'BLOCKING'.

CANVAS/KIT NAME:

Designer:

Purchased from:

Canvas mesh size:

STITCHES:

THREADS:

FINISHING OPTIONS:

NOTES:

TIP: USE A BOX FRAME TO DISPLAY YOUR NEEDLEPOINT MASTERPIECE; THE CANVAS DOESN'T TOUCH THE GLASS AND THIS HELPS TO KEEP YOUR STITCHING FREE FROM ANY MOISTURE.

CANVAS/KIT NAME:

Designer:

Purchased from:

Canvas mesh size:

STITCHES:

THREADS:

FINISHING OPTIONS:

NOTES:

WHO WILL YOU GIVE THIS FINISHED PROJECT TO? WILL IT BECOME A FAMILY HEIRLOOM OR A SPECIAL GIFT FOR A FRIEND? AND WHAT WILL YOU STITCH NEXT?

USING THE GRID PAGES

Whatever your choice of background and filling stitches, you may find yourself in need of some compensating stitches. But what do we mean by compensating stitches?

Compensating stitches enable you to neatly finish right up to the edge of a shaped section. Sometimes, however, there isn't room to use the whole of the stitch, so you have to adapt the working of the stitch to use a partial section of it to finish off.

Compensating stitches can often feel a little bit scary, so when in doubt, take a pencil and draw your defined edge onto the grid paper provided here, and then sketch out how your stitch will travel towards it. This can really help you to visualize what you're up against as you take to the canvas. It's another great way to empower yourself as a stitcher. Trust me, there's nothing you can't tackle!

Soon you'll have the confidence to start creating stitches of your own, and that's another good use for these grid paper pages, sketching out your stitch ideas!

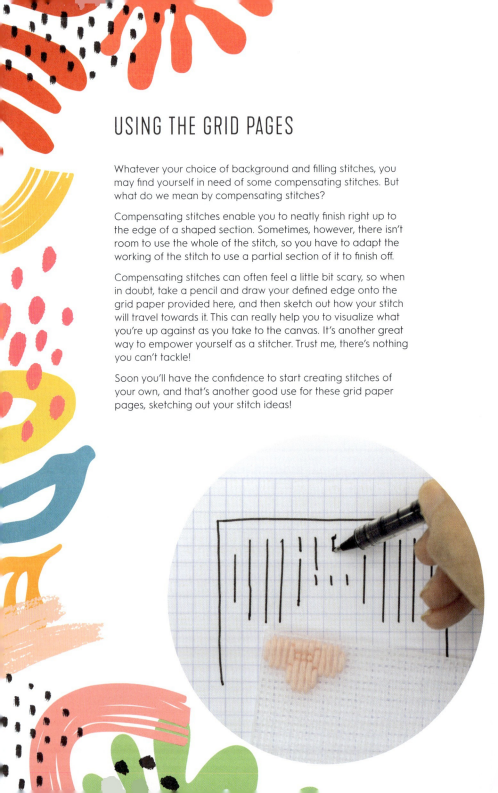

A DAVID AND CHARLES PUBLICATION
© David and Charles, Ltd 2025

David and Charles is an imprint of David and Charles, Ltd
Suite A, Tourism House, Pynes Hill, Exeter, EX2 5WS

Text and Designs © Emma Homent 2025
Layout and Photography © David and Charles, Ltd 2025

First published in the UK and USA in 2025

Emma Homent has asserted her right to be identified as author of this work in accordance with the Copyright, Designs and Patents Act, 1988.

All rights reserved. No part of this publication may be reproduced in any form or by any means, electronic or mechanical, by photocopying, recording or otherwise, without prior permission in writing from the publisher.

Readers are permitted to reproduce any of the designs in this publication for their personal use and without the prior permission of the publisher. However, the designs in this publication are copyright and must not be reproduced for resale.

The author and publisher have made every effort to ensure that all the instructions in the publication are accurate and safe, and therefore cannot accept liability for any resulting injury, damage or loss to persons or property, however it may arise.

A catalogue record for this publication is available from the British Library.

ISBN-13: 9781446315347 paperback

This publication has been printed on paper from approved suppliers and made from pulp from sustainable sources.

Printed in China through Asia Pacific Offset for:
David and Charles, Ltd
Suite A, Tourism House, Pynes Hill, Exeter, EX2 5WS

10 9 8 7 6 5 4 3 2 1

David and Charles publishes high-quality books on a wide range of subjects. For more information visit www.davidandcharles.com.

Share your makes with us on social media using #dandcbooks and follow us on Facebook and Instagram by searching for @dandcbooks.